Yellow Umbrella Books are published by Capstone Press
151 Good Counsel Drive, P.O. Box 669, Mankato, Minnesota 56002
http://www.capstone-press.com

Copyright © 2001 Capstone Press. All rights reserved.
No part of this book may be reproduced without written permission
from the publisher. The publisher takes no responsibility for the use of any
of the materials or methods described in this book, nor for the products thereof.
Printed in the United States of America.

Library of Congress Cataloging-in-Publication Data
Trumbauer, Lisa, 1963–
    Our favorite things to do/by Lisa Trumbauer; consulting editor, Gail Saunders-Smith.
    p. cm.
    Includes index.
    ISBN 0-7368-0739-X
    1. Leisure—Juvenile literature. 2. Recreation—Juvenile literature. 3. Amusements—
Juvenile literature. [1. Amusements.] I. Saunders-Smith, Gail. II. Title.
GV182.9 .T78   2001
790.1'922—dc21   00-036490

    Summary: Describes favorite activities, such as singing, dancing, painting, cooking,
    and camping.

Editorial Credits:
Susan Evento, Managing Editor/Product Development; Elizabeth Jaffe, Senior Editor;
    Charles Hunt, Designer; Kimberly Danger and Heidi Schoof, Photo Researchers

Photo Credits:
Cover: Unicorn Stock Photos/Tom McCarthy; Title Page: International Stock/Chuck Mason;
Page 2: Unicorn Stock Photos/Tom McCarthy; Page 3: Kent & Donna Dannen (top), Index
Stock Imagery (bottom); Page 4: Pictor (top), Index Stock Imagery (bottom); Page 5: Pictor;
Page 6: Shaffer Photography/James L. Shaffer; Page 7: Unicorn Stock Photos/Marie Mills; Page
8: Kent & Donna Dannen (top), Visuals Unlimited/Jeff Greenberg (bottom); Page 9: Unicorn
Stock Photos/Eric Berndt; Page 10: Unicorn Stock Photos/Aneal Vohra; Page 11: Visuals
Unlimited/Inga Spence (top), Photo Network/Myrleen Ferguson Cate (bottom); Page 12:
Unicorn Stock Photos/Jeff Greenberg; Page 13: Index Stock Imagery (left), Index Stock Imagery
and/Bob Winsett (right); Page 14: Photo Network/Bachmann (top), Photri-Microstock/Tom
McCarthy (bottom); Page 15: Pictor (left), International Stock/Mark Bolster (right); Page 16:
Kent & Donna Dannen

1 2 3 4 5 6 06 05 04 03 02 01

Our Favorite Things To Do

By Lisa Trumbauer

Consulting Editor: Gail Saunders-Smith, Ph.D.
Consultants: Claudine Jellison and Patricia Williams,
Reading Recovery Teachers
Content Consultant: Tammy Huber, Youth Education Director,
North Dakota Farmers Union

Yellow Umbrella Books

an imprint of Capstone Press
Mankato, Minnesota

What are your
favorite things to do?
Do you like to play?
Do you like to make things?
Do you like to learn things?

math

Some kids
like music.
They like
to sing.
They like
to play
instruments.

3

Some kids like art.
They like to paint.
They like to make things.

Some kids like to write.
They like to write stories.
They like to write
letters to friends.

Some kids like computers.
They like to do their work
on computers.
They like to play games
on computers.

Some kids like to cook.
They like to mix.
They like to eat
what they make.

Some kids like to go camping.
They like to be outdoors.
They like to hike.

Some kids like to build.
They like to measure.
They like to hammer.

Some kids like to dance.
They like to move to music.
They like to dress up.

Some kids like to play.
They like to play soccer.
They like to ride bikes.

Some kids like to be
with animals.
They like to play with them.
They like to take care of them.

21020

Some kids like to play
in the snow.
They like to make snowmen.
They like to go sledding.

Some kids like to be
in the water.
They like to swim.
They like to splash.

Some kids like to learn
new things.
They like to learn
about rocks.
They like to learn
about dinosaurs.

What are your favorite things to do?

Words to Know/Index

computer—an electronic machine that can store information; page 6

dance—to move in time to music; page 10

dinosaur—any of a group of large reptiles that lived on land in prehistoric times; page 15

favorite—liked the best; pages 2, 16

hammer—to hit a nail with a tool that has a metal head on a handle; page 9

hike—to take a long walk, especially in the country or in the forest; page 8

instrument—an object used to make music; page 3

letter—a written message sent by mail; page 5

measure—to find out the exact size or weight of something; page 9

mix—to stir different things together; page 7

paint—to use a special liquid to make a picture or color a surface; page 4

soccer—a game played by two teams; each team tries to score by kicking a ball into goals at each end of a field; page 11

splash—to throw a liquid; page 14

Word Count: 241
Early-Intervention Levels: 9–12